Original title:
If Life Is a Journey, I've Missed My Exit

Copyright © 2025 Creative Arts Management OÜ
All rights reserved.

Author: Ronan Whitfield
ISBN HARDBACK: 978-1-80566-076-7
ISBN PAPERBACK: 978-1-80566-371-3

Compasses That Point to Nowhere

A map in hand, I took a chance,
But ended up in quite a dance.
I turned around, retraced my steps,
And found a cat who looked perplexed.

I asked the dog for some advice,
He barked and said, "Not once, but twice!"
The tree agreed, it shook its leaves,
While squirrels snickered at my grieves.

The signs all point to left and right,
Yet somehow I'm still lost tonight.
A taco truck could be my guide,
I'll follow scents, I won't abide.

The road ahead is paved with snacks,
With laughter echoing, no time for lacks.
I might not know where I should go,
But I'll enjoy the twists and show.

The Winding Path of Regret

I packed my bags with a cheerful grin,
But forgot the map, oh where to begin?
I took a left at the corner of 'whoops',
And now I'm lost with a herd of goose loops.

The road was bumpy, the signs unclear,
I waved at a cow that just stood there.
With every detour, I found a new snack,
But I still can't figure how to get back.

Detours in Daydreams

I dream of beaches, bright skies above,
But I'm stuck with roads that I can't shove.
Mapped out my chaos with crayons and cheer,
Now I'm sipping coffee at this strange idea.

I thought I'd find fun in each twist and turn,
But it seems I just added a few more concerns.
With GPS off, I'm just following fate,
And wondering if I'll discover a plate.

Uncharted Routes of Reflection

My compass points north, but it's a mystery,
I took the scenic route, a whirlwind history.
Finding lost socks and that odd shoe,
I think I took a left when I meant to go through.

With quirky landmarks along my way,
Like a giant ball of yarn, what a display!
I pause for selfies, the journey's unclear,
Yet every wrong turn brings laughter and cheer.

Lost Between Directions

A sign says 'here' but I'm not so sure,
I'm light on my feet, but heavy on the lure.
It's not a crisis, a cackling delight,
As I stumble through towns, lost in the night.

With each wrong twist, there's a story to tell,
Like the time I serenaded a cow in a spell.
Every step forward feels a bit out of place,
But oh, what a party in this crazy race!

When the GPS Goes Awry

My compass spins like a dancer,
A map full of curls, what a prancer!
Turns out I'm stuck in a loop,
With landmarks that look like soup.

Recalculating, still lost in the fray,
I'm pretty sure I saw that tree yesterday.
U-turns we make, oh what a delight,
Who knew roads could put up such a fight!

Reconciling with the Missed Path

I waved goodbye to that last traffic sign,
Thinking, "What's the rush? I'll be just fine."
Now I'm here, stuck in a pickle,
Wondering why detours are such a trickle.

Should I ask for directions from a duck?
Or trust the whispers of old roadside luck?
Each mile I claw, each turn I fry,
Perhaps it's fate making me comply.

Detours and Destinies

A shortcut turned lengthy — it can't be true!
I'm on the scenic route, just me and my shoe.
Lost in the wild with a bag of snacks,
Making friends with bugs, I'll get no more hacks.

The map's gone rogue, plotting on its own,
Guess I'll write a book on the roads I have shone.
Every twist and turn like a circus parade,
Who knew misadventures could be such a trade?

Remnants of Hues Under the Roadlights

Under neon flickers, my journey unfolds,
Each car that zooms by has stories untold.
I sip my coffee, reflections dance bright,
In this urban canvas, I've lost my flight.

Splashes of color grace each fading scene,
While I chuckle softly, feeling quite keen.
The laughter I share with the shadows I meet,
Turns my missteps into something sweet.

The Weight of Untraveled Options

A map with routes I never chose,
Each road a tale that nobody knows.
I've packed my bags, but stayed in place,
Adventures wave from another space.

The GPS says, 'Turn around, my friend,'
But who knew wandering had no end?
While lost in thoughts beneath the sun,
I laugh at paths I've never run.

Roadside Reflections on Time

Clock ticks slow as I sip my tea,
Bumper-to-bumper, it's just me.
I wave to clouds that drift on by,
Wondering how far I can fly.

With every honk, a story unfolds,
Each driver's dream, a tale untold.
Am I late or right on cue?
Traffic lights turn, but what's my view?

Stolen Moments in a Traffic Jam

Sitting still in a moving line,
Counting how many snacks are mine.
A dance with fate in a metal box,
I break a smile as I eat my socks.

The radio plays my childhood song,
Though deep inside, it feels all wrong.
I wave to strangers, we share a grin,
Time crawling like a state fair spin.

Colliding with My Own Reflections

Mirrors reflect what I can't escape,
A funny face caught in a drape.
Bumping thoughts, they clash and swirl,
Who knew chaos could make me twirl?

As I navigate this wobbly life,
Jesting with fate, avoiding strife.
Each turn I take, a laugh's around,
In the traffic of dreams, I'm glory-bound.

Signs That Led Me Astray

The sign said 'Turn right soon',
I turned left and sang a tune.
My map has coffee stains galore,
Yet I keep searching for the door.

The GPS just lost its mind,
Rerouting me, it seemed so kind.
But every road I wandered down,
Led me back to the same old town.

Bumps on the Road of Intention

Hopped in the car with big bright dreams,
But my engine coughed and burst at the seams.
Potholes danced like they were grand,
Made my coffee spill, isn't that grand?

Traffic signs began to twerk,
As I tried to find my work.
Each little bump I hit with glee,
Cracked the engine, laughed at me!

The Unsung Song of My Detour

Singing loud a tune of bliss,
Ignoring streets that I might miss.
Each twist and turn a brand new song,
With every note, I felt so wrong.

Yet in the chaos of my path,
I found the river, skipped the bath.
Dancing on the roadside green,
In my own weird, lovely scene.

Paths of Dust and Dilemma

Off the beaten path I strayed,
Where dust bunnies danced and played.
Lost my way, but found some fun,
Chasing shadows, in the sun.

What's an exit? Who needs a sign?
I'll sip my drink and whine.
In this maze where I reside,
I'll wear my badge of mischief with pride!

Paths of the Undiscovered Self

I took a left when I should've gone right,
Now I'm stuck in a maze, it feels quite contrite.
The map's upside down, oh what a sight,
With GPS voices, I argue all night.

I ended up lost in a town made of cheese,
The locals all laugh, they say, "Take it with ease!"
I follow the smell of grilled toast on the breeze,
But churning my own butter? Oh please, oh please!

Grains of Time Lost in the Dusty Trails

I packed my bags with socks full of holes,
Chased after a train, but it left with my goals.
The ticket I bought? It was meant for the moles,
Leading me down to a land of lost shoals.

I tripped on a rock, and found my old fears,
Here's a map with directions, but no one appears.
With a compass of gum that has stuck through the years,
Will I ever go forward? I'll drown in my tears!

The Ghosts That Haunt the Highways

They say the road bends where the lost spirits roam,
I swear I've met them, they invited me home.
But their idea of fun? Was to spin and to comb,
Through the endless detours, I felt so alone.

With phantoms I dance at the edge of the lane,
They showed me their tricks but forgot to explain.
The jokes that they make always bring me such pain,
Yet I laugh through the night while they whisper my name!

A Journey in the Threads of Time

Time's like a sweater, unraveling fast,
I knit with bad yarn, just to make it last.
Each stitch goes awry, as I slip and I blast,
A fashion disaster, it's a colorful cast.

Jumping through moments, I miss all the beats,
In shoes properly tied, but never the fleets.
I'll wear mismatched socks and enjoy all the treats,
While plotting my comeback, to a rhythm that repeats!

Veils of Untrodden Trails

I packed my bags with flair and charm,
But left my map, oh what a harm!
The roads were wild, the signs unclear,
I think I took a wrong turn here.

I danced with goats and tripped on rocks,
I lost my phone while counting cocks.
The GPS just laughed and winked,
It led me to a place I blinked.

I tried to climb a hill so steep,
But tumbled down like a ball of sheep.
The views were great, but I got lost,
Adventure's fun, but what's the cost?

So here I am, with stories grand,
A traveler without a planned land.
Next time I'll follow signs, I swear,
But first, I'll stop for ice cream there!

Footprints in the Mist

My footprints danced where clouds did play,
I lost my shoes miles on the way.
The fog rolled in, a sneaky beast,
While I just wanted a simple feast.

I stumbled forth, arms flailing wide,
And knocked a seagull from its stride.
It squawked at me, quite out of place,
As I tripped o'er my own shoelace.

Each path I took turned to a twist,
In search of sunshine, I found a mist.
But laughter followed, how could I fuss?
With memories made from every bus!

So here's to paths that play tricks on me,
To storms that hide what I should see.
With steps so silly, I can't resist,
I'll dance through life, even in the mist!

The Fork That Wasn't Chosen

At every fork, I threw a coin,
But still, the paths got me all torn.
Left or right, I'd spin and shout,
While squirrels laughed and walked about.

I thought I'd take the scenic route,
But ended up in a piggy suit!
With every twist, a brand new mess,
A picnic planned turned to a stress.

The compass spun like it had fun,
Map upside down, I'm on the run!
I followed signs for pizza pie,
But landed in a haystack's sky.

So heed this tale of choices missed,
Life's a ride and I insist!
Next time I'll just stay at home,
And ditch the roads of wild unknown.

A Journey Half-Finished

My suitcase full, oh what a sight,
Yet somehow, I forgot daylight.
A half-done map, a crooked smile,
I've wandered off for quite a while.

With snacks I've packed for days untold,
But only crumbs to now unfold.
I chased a butterfly, how charming!
Then got distracted, oh, so alarming!

The clock struck noon, I lost my way,
In a garden where gnomes play.
They giggled loud and held their sides,
As I searched for my lost ride.

So here's my tale of missed designs,
Of paths that fork and twist in lines.
Though half the journey feels a mess,
Each laugh along the way's a YES!

Omens on the Open Road

Drifting on the highway, birds take flight,
A rubber goose appears, what a sight!
A signpost reads 'U-Turn,' but I'm too late,
My GPS now thinks I'm on a dinner date.

Potholes like craters, my shocks just squeal,
Coffee cup spills, an oily wheel deal.
A raccoon's my co-pilot, what a fun ride,
With snacks and a nap, we take it in stride.

Billboards scream loudly, what's their appeal?
One claims I'll win big, but I just can't feel.
A giant hotdog waves, his mustard so bright,
Yet I just want directions, not a food fight.

The exit signs giggle, they dance all around,
But when I reach for them, they won't be found.
With each turn of the wheel, I just can't quite see,
This roadside comedy that's living in me.

Whispers of the Highway's End

Onward I drive, but where is my goal?
An old man's laughing, parked in a shoal.
His lawn gnome grins, keeps nudging me here,
While I fumble with maps like I've got a fear.

Each lane tells a story, or so they proclaim,
But I simply wander, forgetting the game.
Curves that are sharp aren't helping my fate,
With each step I take, I just tempt my fate.

The roundabouts spin, like a dizzying dance,
Twirling my sanity, losing my chance.
A squirrel with sunglasses shows me some flair,
Yet I'm just a traveler lost in midair.

I'm running late, or maybe I'm not,
Either way, I'll blame all the laughs that I've got.
It's all in the journey, they often will say,
But I just want to know where it went astray.

Forks in the Road

A sign points left, and one veers right,
Forks in the road cause quite a fright.
Do I head to the beach or a ghostly town?
I'll pick the one where they serve ice cream down.

But lo! A detour looms in the haze,
My stomach grumbles, adding to the craze.
I swear I saw a cactus wearing a hat,
Telling me secrets while I sit and chat.

Maps folded poorly, I'm lost in a maze,
Chasing a llama that's lost in a daze.
Yet with every misstep, I giggle and cheer,
For this wild ride's just a comic sphere.

Now I see a sign "Y'all turn around!"
In a pickle jar rattle, I make my confound.
Yet here in the silly, I've found the right way,
Forks in my path always lead me to play.

Missed Turns and Overtures

Turning the wheel was a grand charade,
Missed my exit, now I'm on a parade.
With clowns and balloons, it's a raucous affair,
Yet all I wanted was a straight freeway glare.

The left turn I took brought me to a fair,
I'm face-to-face with a grinning bear.
With cotton candy and laughter around,
I'm still wondering how I got unbound.

Ding-dong! The doorbell's my next cue,
A marching band jives as I bid adieu.
My travel log's filled with giggles and blips,
With a map of confusion and candy-coated trips.

I might have missed signaling, too keen to fly,
But with laughs filling highways, oh my, oh my!
With every wrong turn, I'll dance and I'll twirl,
For life's not a goal, it's a goofy whirl.

The Scenic View of Missed Chances

I took a wrong turn, oh what a delight,
My GPS laughs; it knows I won't fight.
Cliffs of bad choices, mountains of doubt,
But the view's pretty good, there's no need to pout.

With snacks in the back and a dog at my feet,
The road's not so bad, it's a comical feat.
Who knew the detours would lead me to this?
A scenic adventure, I can't help but grinning bliss.

A Pathway Paved with Hesitation

I paused at the fork when I shouldn't have stayed,
A lifetime of wondering, decisions delayed.
The squirrels are judging, their chatter's too loud,
But I'm quite content in this curious crowd.

I twiddle my thumbs, my plans in a mess,
Yet, I've never seen nature wear quite so much zest.
The pathways are twisted, oh what a sight,
Who needs a straight path when absurd is so right?

Stranded in a Parallel Realm

Lost in a world where clocks like to play,
Ticking and tocking, but I've gone astray.
Butterflies chatter, they seem so confused,
I'm stuck in a loop, and I'm not even bruised.

I wave to the shadows, they wave back in glee,
They welcomed me here, said 'Stay for some tea.'
We'll talk about choices, the roads we forgot,
And laugh at the moments I swear I have shot.

Delays on the Journey of Self

With a ticket in hand for the train that won't come,
I sit on the platform, but I'm far from done.
People rush past, their purpose so clear,
While I sip my coffee, enjoying the cheer.

I've missed all the stops, but hey, what a view,
The barista now knows me; I think we're a crew.
So here's to the halts that let us unwind,
In a line for life's circus, I've truly aligned.

The Unraveled Map

In the depths of my glove box,
Lay a map, all crumpled and wrinkled,
Once it showed great adventures,
Now it's just a jigsaw, all twinkled.

I thought I'd take a shortcut,
But turned onto a road less traveled,
Now I'm stuck behind some cows,
While my great plan has sadly unraveled.

Each turn leads to more confusion,
GPS just giggles and sighs,
With each wrong turn I make,
I'm the king of failed tries!

Oh, what I'd give for a sign,
That points towards my own ol' house,
But these twists and silly turns,
Have me feeling like just a louse!

A Ticket for Tomorrow

In my pocket, slips a ticket,
For a train I've missed, oh dear!
The conductor just rolled his eyes,
As I waved goodbye with cheer.

Next one's in a hundred minutes,
I might as well have a drink,
I ordered coffee, spicy tacos,
Never thought I'd have time to think.

With crumbs on my lap and a smile,
'What a ride,' I can only say,
They'll call me the 'Ticket Master,'
When I sleep here the rest of the day.

But at least I'll have this story,
About the time I lost my way,
Through food and fun, I'll remember,
How to travel, or just delay!

The Path That Lies Ahead

Looking forward, the path is fuzzy,
With road signs pointing the wrong way,
I squint and ponder my options,
Chasing squirrels, I think I'll stay.

Maps and apps just conspire,
To lead me down paths askew,
Sidestepping puddles and mysteries,
I blame it all on their review.

The man in front looks lost too,
He's dancing with a shopping cart,
We might just start a brigade,
To find where the real fun starts.

Winding roads can be amusing,
Check your shoes for a surprise,
With laughter echoing behind us,
The destination's in our minds!

Shadows of Forgotten Roads

In the shadows of quaint highways,
Where my ambitions took a rest,
I wander with a lingering chuckle,
Wondering which route is the best.

A detour past the ice cream truck,
When sunny skies dropped a rain,
Now I'm splashing with my thoughts,
Laughing at life's little pain.

Each street a puzzle, a riddle,
With memories clinging like glue,
I find joy in misadventures,
While the world flips a coin anew.

So here I stand, confused but smiling,
As the shadows dance with glee,
Every wrong turn's a story,
Of roads that just weren't meant for me!

Resurfaced Reflections at the Junction

I'm driving on a whim, oh what a ride,
With coffee in my hand, I take it in stride.
The GPS whispers, 'Turn left at the bee,'
But I zoomed right past—now where could I be?

The stop sign's a riddle, I've never decoded,
Each blink of the signal leaves me overloaded.
Road signs are laughing, it's all quite absurd,
As I chase my lost dreams with each wacky word.

I take a detour through the town of regret,
With a map made of ice cream, how could I fret?
There's a circus of thoughts that never make sense,
Oh, I signed up for thrills, but the ride's pretty dense!

Now I'm at a crossroads, expect some confusion,
Should I go for adventure or just grab a fusion?
The laughter gets louder, my heart gives a leap,
In this whimsical world, I'm lost but I'll keep!

The Forgotten Fork in the Dreams

In a land where forks wear hats and play cards,
I made my decision, but it seemed quite hard.
Choosing between spaghetti and a slice of pie,
But either way, let's just give it a try!

Oh, the plants are all nodding, giving me hints,
But my logic's eloping, and it's making no sense.
While the soup's getting colder and the bread starts to dance,
In this culinary quest, there's no second chance.

As the clock ticks away, I race with delight,
The dessert has a spark that could light up the night.
But wait, there's a banana that's wanting a word,
It says, "Stay at my side; together we'll herd!"

So here's to spooning and twirling our fate,
In this kitchen of dreams, let's just celebrate!
The dishes are laughing, the table's a show,
And even if I'm lost, just let the fun flow!

Twilight Mist on Abandoned Avenues

Under twilight's gaze, the streetlights hum,
With mist in the air, where's the beat of the drum?
I wander past shadows where memories sprout,
Each block holds a secret, but I'm filled with doubt.

Bicycles whisper as they zoom past my feet,
"Where is the magic? Isn't this quite a feat?"
Laughter erupts from an old rusty swing,
While I chase after echoes that life used to bring.

The benches are storytellers wearing old hats,
In this realm of the quirky, like whimsical chats.
"Step back, have some fun, leave behind your woes,"
But I laugh at the thought, because anything goes!

So I twirl with the breeze, let my worries dissolve,
In this maze of the night where the quirky evolve.
Even if I misstep, the stars give a wink,
In avenues dark, there's joy in the blink.

When the Undertow of Fate Pulls You Under

Caught in a wave, my compass spins 'round,
With the ocean of choices, I'm completely bound.
I packed all my hopes in a suitcase too small,
As the tides play charades, I just giggle and sprawl.

The surf is confusing, it swirls and it sways,
I'm tossed like a leaf in a wild, dancey maze.
But there's humor in chaos, so I start to create,
A sandcastle kingdom—let's celebrate fate!

Encountering mermaids who sing in the foam,
I'm swept by the currents to a whimsical home.
They offer me seashells, wave crystal and cheer,
I think I'll stay here, let's toast with a beer!

As the undertow pulls, I'll ride out the fun,
In the whirlpools of life, we're never outrun.
With laughter as my life vest, I sail through the sea,
Even if I'm submerged, I'll be wild and free!

Lost Along the Byways

I took a wrong turn, oh what a surprise,
The GPS chuckled, it had rolled its eyes.
Traffic cones danced, roadside signs mocked,
I waved at the cows, they too, seemed shocked.

Found an old diner with a menu that's stuck,
Guess I'll have pancakes, or maybe just luck.
The waitress just winked, said, "That'll be fine!"
While I counted my change, it was all just a dime.

Wandered through fields where the daisies bloom,
A sign says 'This Way,' but I feel such gloom.
I stopped for a selfie, my hair all a mess,
The cows photobombed, adding to the stress.

Stumbling through life on this odd little route,
With squirrels as my guides in their fuzzy old suits.
Lost along the highways, I'll never complain,
For laughter is gold in this silly old game.

Detours of the Heart

A map full of love, but the road is a twist,
I took the wrong exit, oh what did I miss?
On my way to romance, I fell into a pond,
Splashing right past where my true love had dawned.

With hearts on the dashboard, I thought I could steer,
But love's traffic lights never quite seem clear.
I honked at the feelings, they waved goodbye,
And I'm stuck at the corner where crushes all lie.

A detour, they said, take the scenic route round,
But all that I found were clowns in the town.
They juggled my hopes while I tried to discern,
That love is a circus, and now I must learn.

So I laughed with the jesters, took note of my fate,
And left with a smile, though love can't wait.
The map may be wrong, but at least it's cute,
In this wild ride of hearts, I'll take the detour to suit.

The Road Not Taken

I stood at a fork, now wasn't that grand?
Two roads before me, neither well planned.
One said 'quick coffee,' the other 'stay late,'
I chose the first and got trapped in a date.

Heard tales of success on a road paved with dreams,
But I found a car wash with questionable beams.
There was soap everywhere, all lathered in foams,
And I drove off with bubbles, not tied to any homes.

The crossroads of life are a marvelous sight,
But the choices are funny, a true comedic light.
I laughed with the seagulls, they squawked back in glee,
And I pondered my future while sipping my tea.

In every misstep, there's a giggle or two,
Just follow the laughter, it'll guide you anew.
The road not taken is wild, don't you see?
Filled with whimsy and wonder, it's perfect for me.

Unseen Crossroads

I stumbled 'cross highways where lost spirits roam,
A sign said 'this way,' but I called it home.
Turns out it was wrong, as I danced with the deer,
They laughed at my journey, then stopped for a cheer.

Found a place called 'Oops!' on this winding lane,
With burgers named 'Regrets' and fries filled with pain.
The waiter just grinned, said, "Join in on the fun!"
I ordered a smile, they said it's on the run.

My compass was spinning, my map had a fit,
But oh, did I chuckle, I couldn't just quit.
Each step was a giggle, a tumble of joy,
At the unseen crossroads, I felt like a boy.

So here's to the paths that lead us astray,
With laughter our guide on this whimsical way.
Unseen but inviting, they whisper, "Let's go!"
Adventures await us, just follow the glow.

Wayfarer Without a Compass

Lost beneath a sky so wide,
I chase my tail like a wayward guide.
The map I bought, all colors bright,
Leads me to places that aren't quite right.

With every turn, a sign goes past,
Saying 'This way!' but it's quite the blast.
Without a clue, I roam about,
The wanderlust has turned to doubt.

I asked a bird for directions near,
It chirped a tune, then flew off in cheer.
Now I'm left with a faded sheet,
And shoes that ache from too much repeat.

In my mishaps, I find the fun,
Chasing shadows beneath the sun.
Though the exit's far, I'll dance, not fret,
A wayfarer's joy, I'd never regret.

Signals in the Fog

Amidst the mist, I squint and strain,
A flicker here, a blip of gain.
The signals flash, I wave goodbye,
To turns I've missed, my oh my!

A cloud of doubt hangs thick like stew,
Directions blurred, it's quite a brew.
To take a left? Or was it right?
My sense of direction takes flight!

I followed a squirrel that seemed so wise,
Only to find it's just after fries.
Giggling to myself, I roam with glee,
Lost in a maze that holds the key.

Yet in this haze, I find delight,
Strange adventures in the fading light.
Though eyes can't see, my heart stays bright,
The journey's the prize, let's dine tonight!

Wandering Off the Beaten Path

Where the roads are paved, I went amiss,
Trekking trails that look like bliss.
I stumbled past a kissing tree,
Hoping for guidance, it just kissed me!

A band of ants offered me toast,
But that's not what I wanted most.
Their tiny chatter, ever so sweet,
Led me astray, but it's quite the feat!

Every twist pulls me further away,
Each dead end feels like a fun ballet.
With chuckles escaping my puzzled lips,
I embrace the chaos with silly flips.

Though I wander far from all that's plain,
In every misstep, there's laughter to gain.
For each wrong turn is a tale to tell,
I'll toast to my flair for the lost and well!

Echoes of Missed Opportunities

Oh, the exits I could've claimed,
Yet here I am, a little ashamed.
Like a pinball bouncing with flair,
Missing chances with ironic care.

I signed up for yoga, missed the week,
Now I'm stretching just to sneak a peek.
The teacher smiles, but I'm confused,
Where's the exit that I've refused?

Once I chased a bus, or so I thought,
Ended up at a dog park, whoops, not!
With furry friends, I wag my doubts,
Canine wisdom, laughter shouts.

Though my chances may fade like a phantasm,
In every blunder, there's a fine chasm.
So here's to missed turns, we share a jest,
In this wild ride, we're truly blessed!

Veering Off the Beaten Track

My GPS grew tired and took a nap,
I ended up in a llama shop wrap.
With fuzzy friends munching on my shoe,
Guess I'll need directions, who knew?

They all looked at me with sheer delight,
As I tried to negotiate the route right.
"I'll pay in carrots," I made my claim,
But it turns out, they don't eat such fame.

Bumbled out feeling quite absurd,
Swiping left on the map, such a blur.
When did my coffee break turn into this?
Adventures like these, you just can't miss!

So here's to the roads we never planned,
With snacks and chuckles, all unscanned.
A detour worth every weird surprise,
Life's a laugh when you improvise!

A Compass of Crumpled Dreams

I bought a compass, shiny and bright,
It pointed left but I turned right.
In search of destiny, I drove so far,
Ended up at a weird pickle bazaar.

Pickles were singing, or so I thought,
In a jarred chorus, they danced and fought.
I asked for directions, they rolled their eyes,
"Try the hot dogs, that's where fun lies!"

With mustard trails leading me astray,
I popped some popcorn, life's buffet.
The compass laughed, "You're doing just fine,
Follow the snacks, you'll never decline!"

So cheers to the dreams that lose their way,
With pickles and popcorn at the buffet.
Let's frolic through the map's silly bends,
When crumpled dreams turn into new friends!

Confessions at the Crosswalk

Standing here, light's red, palms sweaty,
Confessions to pigeons? Yep, I'm ready.
"I swear I saw you cross the street,
That was my sandwich! We could have met!"

But here I am, talking to birds,
Spilling the beans, no judgment, just words.
"Can you fly me home, oh feathered crew?
I promise I'll share my socks, yes, it's true!"

The walk signal changes, I'm feeling bold,
Time to trot, let the stories unfold.
Yet here I linger, caught in the chat,
With pigeons as pals, how about that?

Oh life, you trickster, with your silly stunts,
Here I stand, making feathered chums.
When confusion's a laugh and laughter's a friend,
Crosswalk confessions, let's not pretend!

Unfollowed Trail of Hopes

I took a path marked 'Great Expectations',
Only to find it led to frustrations.
A signpost showed a picture of cake,
But all I discovered was an old lake.

With hopes unfollowed like pesky ads,
I searched for smiles but found just fads.
"Join the fun!" said a squirrel in a vest,
But he left me hanging, what a jest!

Lost in this hike of missed opportunities,
Swapping my dreams for squirrels' communities.
Yet amid the giggles and trails gone wrong,
Turns out awkward just might be where I belong!

So here's to the paths we wander awry,
With squirrels and gigs, I'll laugh till I cry.
In a world of missteps and hope that men,
I'll create my fun; let the stories begin!

Remnants of a Faded Trail

I took a turn at the last street sign,
Thought it led to a party, felt mighty fine.
Instead, I found a cow, chewing grass,
Looked at me like, "Buddy, you really should pass!"

My map was a puzzle, pieces all lost,
Every twist and turn had a heavy cost.
I honked at a goose, it strutted with flair,
Guess it knew the route—I just wanted to share!

Curves and ruts, what a merry chase,
Tangled up in laughter, forgot my place.
Each bump in the road, a dance of delight,
Should've brought snacks for this wild, wobbly flight!

So here I stand, with my cap askew,
On a highway to nowhere, with a view quite askew.
In this muddled maze, I can clearly see,
The sign says, "Welcome to Comedic Misery!"

The Last Farewell to Waypoints

Every waypoint I missed, did a silly little jig,
I waved to the GPS, said, "You're a big pig!"
It laughed at my antics, my wrong turns, my fate,
While I groaned and chuckled, it was far too late.

Sailed past a diner with donuts galore,
Thought about stopping, but who's counting the score?
Life's full of detours, this much I know,
But do they serve fries at this roadside show?

Misread the signs, oh what a mess,
Found myself caught in a colorful dress.
The locals just stared, as I waved in retreat,
"Nice outfit!" they shouted, while I shuffled my feet.

So farewell to the markers I deemed important,
Now I search for a taco truck, oh, how I'm wanting!
As the sun sets, I ponder my spree,
Maybe the best detours were just meant for me!

Unfolding Routes of Regret

Map in hand, I thought I was sly,
But all I could find was a chicken and pie.
Regret painted my face, like a day-old scare,
At this intersection where no one else was there.

The road not taken was a crackerjack,
With twists so tight, I thought I'd fall back.
I choked on my laughter, spilled coffee on my lap,
Instead of smooth sailing, I hit every gap.

I asked a raccoon for direction and flair,
He pointed to nowhere, then gave me a stare.
Mapping my journey, turned into a jest,
All roads lead to fun, and this one's the best!

So here I stand, covered in crumbs,
With the echoes of laughter and leftover sums.
Routes of regret? More like routes of glee,
In this funny old maze, I found the real me!

Reflections in a Pothole

In the puddle of a pothole, my dreams were afloat,
Reflections of mishaps in a rusty old boat.
"Where to next?" I asked, with a grin so wide,
As waves of laughter took me for a ride.

I turned too sharp, like a swan in a race,
Instead of a highway, ended up with a face.
In the mirror of mischief, I could see it clear,
All my wrong turns were triggering cheer!

With each bump and thud, the comedic delight,
Wobbling and giggling turned wrong into right.
So let's celebrate chaos with a toast, a cheer,
In the deeper the pothole, the fun's drawing near!

So here's to the laughs and the twists that we take,
Every fumbled mistake just adds to the cake.
In puddles of life, may we always see,
The mirrors of joy in our own quirky spree!

Missed Landmarks on the Map of Dreams

I was driving with my eyes closed, slowly lost,
Detours made me a tourist, at a great cost.
I saw a roadside stand, selling dreams on a plate,
But my GPS said 'Recalculating'—what a fate!

Sipped on a smoothie of 'maybe' and 'what if,'
Drove past my goals like they were a myth.
Every sign was a laugh, a chuckle, a jest,
The road to success? I simply guessed best!

Found a billboard that read, 'Success is near!'
But I forgot to stop for directions, I fear.
I took the wrong exit, a path paved in ruts,
Now I'm driving in circles—ain't life full of guts?

So here I sit with my sandwich of doubt,
Auto-pilot on, and I'm still figuring out.
Next time I'll read the signs, take my time,
For missing the markers? Well, it seems it's a crime!

Reflections in the Rearview

Looking back through the glass of the past,
I see my chances, oh they're fading fast.
Riding through memories in a clunky old car,
I'm lost in a mist, like a dusty old star.

Laughing at the times I took lefts instead of rights,
Trying to catch the quicksilver of nights.
A parade of mishaps, oh the stories I weave,
But I'm the clown at the circus—ready to leave!

The roads were so winding, the bumps never few,
And I picked up a hitchhiker named 'Regret', too.
But we sang silly songs, made a great little team,
Driving to places I swore were a dream.

So here's to the trips that didn't go planned,
With a mix of confusion and laughter so grand.
I'll cherish the chaos, the moments that flare,
With a rearview of giggles, I haven't a care!

Whispers of the Directions Not Taken

An old map unfolded, a riddle in disguise,
Each line a laugh, each fold a surprise.
Took a right when I should have just stayed home,
Now I'm lost in a maze of bubblegum foam.

The voice in the GPS sounded a bit coy,
It chuckled and said, 'Enjoy all the joy.'
I waved to my dreams in the lane next to mine,
While I'm stuck here picking daisies, good line!

I asked for advice from a squirrel in a tree,
It shrugged and it laughed, 'Life's all about glee!'
So I danced with misfortune, twirled through the clover,
Who knew that my stumbles could make me feel bolder?

With every twist taken, a punchline in disguise,
I banter with fate, as humor just flies.
These whispers of paths not taken today,
Turn out to be giggles that light up my way!

Missteps in the Dance of Time

Two left feet on this dance floor of fate,
Trip over the rhythm, oh, isn't it great?
The clock keeps on ticking, but I'm out of sync,
Should I tango with dreams, or just play at the brink?

Twirling with laughter, stepping on toes,
Skipped every beat, as everybody knows.
A waltz turned to cha-cha, I'm lost in the sound,
Bumping into moments where laughter is found.

I twirl in the spotlight, a clown in disguise,
With the world as my audience, they roll their eyes.
Yet I take each misstep with a grin ear to ear,
After all, life's just a dance full of cheer.

And as the music fades into sweet twilight,
I'll keep on dancing, oh, what a sight!
For every misstep, my heart finds a rhyme,
In the dance of existence, I'm winning through time!

Uncharted Directions

Map in hand, oh what a sight,
My GPS took a flight.
Left the road I thought I knew,
Now I'm lost, who knew?

Unexpected turns and bends,
Laughing with my new best friends.
A llama camp, a taco stand,
Guess I'll just make my own plan.

The gas light flickers, what a tease,
Running on empty, yet at ease.
I'll dance in circles, make it fun,
Who needs an exit? I'll just run!

Sudden detours, come what may,
Life's a game, let's laugh and play.
In this chaos, joy I find,
Adventure calls, I'm not left behind.

When Time Lost Its Way

Tick tock, where did it go?
Hours vanished, just like snow.
I thought I'd age like fine wine,
But I feel more like sour brine.

Years have slipped through fingers tight,
Trying to catch them, what a sight!
Clock hands dance without a care,
While I'm stuck in this old chair.

Cancel the plans, can't find my phone,
Lost in time, yet not alone.
Let's race the sunrise, take a chance,
Who needs a schedule for this dance?

Next week's meeting? What's that for?
I'd rather nap and explore some more.
Time's a trickster, let it be,
I'll get there eventually… or not, you see!

Beneath the Weight of Choices

Menus piled high, oh dear me,
Do I want soup or a tree?
Forks and knives in chaos reign,
Too many choices drive me insane.

Exit stage left? That sounds great,
But what if I choose to wait?
A chocolate cake calls out my name,
Do I play it safe, or join the game?

Future paths turned into mazes,
I wear my doubts like funny phrases.
Do I suit up or wear my jeans?
Life's just a riddle, or so it seems.

Oh choices, sweet contradiction,
In every turn, there's a new fiction.
With each decision, I laugh and sigh,
Guess I'll just wing it, oh me, oh my!

The Scenic Route to Nowhere

Taking the long way, blissful cheer,
While my destination disappears.
Roadside attractions catch my eye,
Do I take the plunge or just drive by?

Every mile feels like a tease,
Stopping for snacks, oh what a breeze!
Slowing down to smell the flowers,
Wasting time builds up my powers.

Accidental stops make the best tales,
Like when I rode a moose in braids and pails.
The map's a joke, so I'll never know,
Where I'm headed, just watch me go!

With laughter loud, I'll steer the wheel,
No one can tell me how to feel.
In this joyride, I'm truly free,
Scenic route? Oh, just let it be!

Memories Woven Into the Grime of the Highway

I thought I'd seen it all today,
But missed the sign—now I'm in dismay.
Chasing sunsets, I lost track of time,
And now I'm stuck, like a half-baked rhyme.

The GPS is singing me a tune,
With reroutes and detours by the light of the moon.
I waved goodbye to the best-laid plans,
Now I'm just the king of traffic jams.

They say, "Stop and smell the roses!"
But I've stopped at every fast food poses.
In a world of choices, I chose the fries,
With a side of regrets in extra-large size.

So here I sit with a soda in hand,
Reflecting on paths I didn't quite plan.
Life's punchlines feel like cruel little jests,
But I'll laugh it off—who needs the rest?

Between Here and Somewhere Else

Stuck between places, I'm on the road,
With my map upside down, and a random code.
Each mile I drive feels like a wild guess,
Finding mysteries in each messy mess.

"Turn left," it says, "No, it's right!" I moan,
Blasting tunes that make me feel all alone.
My coffee's cold but I'm still awake,
Wondering which exit was the big mistake.

A buffet of choices spreads through my brain,
But all I find is a growing disdain.
I could've had tacos, but chose just a bun,
Now I'm in a taco-shaped run and run!

The laughter echoes through my rearview glass,
As my choices parade like a clumsy brass.
Adventure calls, but I'm still parked here,
With my heart on my sleeve and a side of beer.

Windswept Landscapes of What-Could-Have-Been

I envisioned a future, bright and so grand,
Instead, I sit with my fries in hand.
Thought I'd be somewhere worth the hype,
But here I am still taking another swipe.

Each turn I take feels like a rerun,
Lost in a maze where I can't find fun.
Got the playlist going, but it's stuck on repeat,
My life's a soundtrack gone obsolete.

I see the highways fork, a thrilling surprise,
And wonder if I'm the prize for the flies.
Oh to soar where the wild winds teem,
But instead, I'm lost in a daydream.

So here's to the laughs as I stall and meander,
Where my wishes float by like driftwood and slander.
Between exits and dreams, we find what we seek,
Even if it's just in a traffic peak!

The Unsung Journey of Yesterdays

Beneath the weight of yesterday's fog,
I wade through memories like a soggy dog.
Driving slow through the ghosts of my past,
Each pothole a story, too wacky to last.

Road signs flash like wishes I ignored,
With destinations I failed to afford.
But here I am, laughing in the fray,
As my life plays tag with a runaway stray.

The map's a doodle, a scribble, a joke,
Leading me down where the wise folks spoke.
I could've taken that left to find fame,
But decided to play the "lost" game.

So cheers to the ride, it's one wild show,
Where punchlines land in a comical flow.
With every missed turn, I twist and I twirl,
In the grand, messy dance of this oddball world.

The Dim Light on the Long Road

The headlights flicker, oh what a sight,
My GPS just said, 'You're doing alright!'
There's a burger joint calling, right up ahead,
But here I am lost, dreams filling my head.

Road signs are waving, but I'm driving blind,
Tried to take shortcuts, but I can't seem to find.
Every twist and turn leads me far, far away,
Maybe I'll take a nap—who needs to play?

I wave at the cows, they stare back at me,
'Is this how you drive?' they seem to decree.
With laughter and jokes, I embrace the absurd,
Navigating life's map feels so very blurred.

The dim light is fading, should I make U-turns?
Or keep on cruising till my stomach churns?
With snacks in my lap, and tunes oh so sweet,
Who needs a destination? This ride is a treat!

Echoing Footsteps of Departed Journeys

I packed up my bags, with snacks galore,
Hit the road with gusto, who could ask for more?
But now I'm just wandering, quite off the trail,
Chasing after echoes, oh what a fail!

Each step that I take, I hear laughter and sighs,
Specters of my choices dancing in disguise.
With ghosts from the past, I share my last fries,
Can't tell what is real through these blurry skies.

The sidewalks are crowded, with memories bright,
But I trip on my laces and lose my delight.
With shoes untied, laughter fills the air,
In the race of my life, I'm stuck in a chair.

As footsteps fade softly, I wave them goodbye,
Feeling a bit silly, I look to the sky.
Here's to the journey, whatever it be,
At least I have stories, and snacks, oh so free!

Anchored in the Harbor of Hesitation

The boat in the harbor is ready to sail,
But I'm on the dock, stuck telling a tale.
With wind in my hair and a drink in my hand,
Fear stops my feet, it's an odd little stand.

I ponder the waves, where shall they go?
With dreams of adventure, but my legs move slow.
The anchor is heavy, my heart feels the weight,
Should I leap on board, or just sit here and wait?

With seagulls a-squawking, they laugh at my plight,
'Come dance with the tide, you'll feel so alright!'
But I sip my lemonade and wave to the shore,
Not sure if I'm ready to open the door.

So here in my harbor, I twiddle my thumbs,
Life's wild sea beckons, but still, I feel numb.
With snacks in my pocket, I giggle and grin,
Maybe tomorrow, I'll finally begin!

The Longing Linger for Lost Exits

Those exits fly by, like a flick of a wing,
I wave as they vanish; oh, the joy they could bring!
With a sigh of regret, I keep on the trail,
My map is a puzzle, a confusing detail.

I dream of a place where the grass grows so lush,
With pizza and puppies, oh, what a rush!
Yet here I remain, in this traffic jam bliss,
Laughing at life's little, whimsical twists.

What was that exit? It slipped my little mind,
Each mile a new riddle, so cleverly designed.
The laughter of friends echo deep in my chest,
I'll cherish these moments, I gratefully jest.

So onward I travel, with humor as my guide,
Making memories sweet as I laugh at the ride.
If the exits are lost, I'll just take my time,
For life is a giggle, and I'm glad to rhyme!

Memories of the Untraveled Path

I packed my bags with care,
Yet forgot my map somewhere.
My GPS lost its signal there,
Now I'm just going in circles, I swear.

I waved to folks I never knew,
Used a roadmap marked in blue.
Each turn I took was quite askew,
Now I'm dining with a kangaroo.

The sights I missed, a grand parade,
Instead, I found a forest glade.
A cow made friends—I felt betrayed,
Befriending cows, my plans delayed.

Each laugh turns into a mile,
My journey's filled with goofy style.
At least I'll leave with stories a while,
And a cow who knows how to smile.

Milestones That Came and Went

I thought I'd hit the grand old gate,
But there's a sign—it's far too late.
I iced my cake, but missed the date,
Now I'm stuck with gifts I can't berate.

Birthday wishes came and went,
A year had passed—what's my intent?
I brought the streamers, whole shebang,

Yet found the party's overhang.

I cheered for turns I could not track,
While riding on an old knickknack.
A milestone passed, I hit the sack,
Had dreams of cheer, but found a quack.

Remembering laughs, I chime along,
Where did it go, my sense of wrong?
In this heap of silly songs,
I find the roads can't be that long.

The Silent Screech of Missed Turns

I swerved right, my map was wrong,
The exit vanished, sang its song.
A silent scream as headlights throng,
The wrong lane feels like where I belong.

I bumbled through each twisty lane,
A parking lot was my big gain.
With every turn, I feel the pain,
Made friends with pigeons—what a reign!

Oh, the missed exits, sigh and frown,
Waving at the folks who've come and gone.
But laughing at myself, I crown,
With a penguin plush that I've found upon.

The tire screech echoes a retreat,
But can't deny the humor's sweet.
In this circus, life's complete,
With every flub, there's more to meet.

A Souvenir From the Wrong Destination

I meant to find a sunny shore,
But ended up with so much more.
A postcard reads of frozen lore,
I guess I'll keep this fridge decor.

I packed my dreams, my beachy style,
Yet ended up at a winter aisle.
Every snowman wears a smile,
While I just needed sun awhile.

Each souvenir, a quirky find,
Socks with penguins all aligned.
My suitcase spills with goods combined,
A wardrobe full of laughs designed.

So here I stand in blizzard's way,
Searching for sun, come what may.
With pizza slices made of clay,
This trip's a memory, come what play.

The Fog Beyond Familiar Signposts

I drove past a sign that said 'Turn here!'
But fog clouded paths that seemed all too clear.
With a map upside down and a GPS glitch,
I found myself lost in quite the strange pitch.

The trees waved hello, or so it appeared,
Like old friends who knew just how I had veered.
In the fog I met squirrels who giggled and danced,
While I was just hoping for a way back, perhaps.

Journey's End: A Pause Unanticipated

I meant to arrive at my destination soon,
Instead, I'm now stuck with a bear and a raccoon.
They pooled all their snacks while I munched on my pride,
Oh to be a man with a map that's not lied!

The raccoon told stories of wild, crazy nights,
While I sipped my coffee, seeing strange lights.
And when all was done, I left full of cheer,
Though my plans went astray, I had fun, it's clear!

Roadblocks on the Route to Myself

Traffic cones littered the road to my goal,
As I swerved to avoid them, I stole a glance, whole.
There stood a sign saying 'Detour! Free donuts!'
If it's not about snacks, am I really that nuts?

Then one cop waved me to the edge of the road,
His donut was gone, oh the irony flowed.
He pointed and laughed, 'Don't take life too tight,'
And I drove off with sprinkles, feeling quite bright.

Abandoned Roads and Altered Plans

Google Maps led me astray with a wink,
Down an abandoned road where the cows came to think.
I waved as they chewed, so peaceful and free,
They seemed more content than just poor old me.

Lost minutes turned hours in the midst of my quest,
With my car now a pasture, looking quite a mess.
Yet I laughed at the cows, as they stared and snorted,
In a detour I found joy, my worries aborted.

Shadows of the Untraveled

In a car with a flat tire, it's quite a show,
My maps say right, but I went left, oh no!
A raccoon waves goodbye as I drive on by,
With a backpack of snacks, it's an impromptu pie.

The GPS talking like a backseat friend,
Recalculating routes that seem to never end.
The road sign's a joke, it points to nowhere fast,
My coffee's gone cold, and these miles are a blast.

A hitchhiker's grin says he's lost like me,
"We should start a club, no map, just glee!"
We swap tales of trips, all the places we missed,
Plan a new route, but just for a twist.

In the rearview, my worries fade away,
Chasing horizons on this wild highway.
So let's laugh at the turns where we lost our way,
Every bump in the road is just part of the play.

Hitches Along the Highway

I took a short trip, or so I declared,
But ended up stranded, a bit unprepared.
The snack stash is empty, not even a crumb,
But here comes a cow, mooing, and looking dumb.

An exit sign glimmers, but it's just a tease,
I pull off for gas, but I'm lost in the trees.
A dog's barking loudly, it's joining my plight,
"Are you lost like me? Let's just stay the night!"

The road trip's a sitcom, each mile is a gag,
My car as a stage, I'm the star of this flag.
With laughter as fuel, I can't complain,
Who needs a destination, when fun's in the lane?

So here's to the hitches and oddball delays,
To laughter and mishaps on these wild, winding ways.
Each moment's a treasure, they're etched in my mind,
In the comedy theater where the road is unkind.

Encounters at Unmarked Stops

At a diner that smells like old frying grease,
I meet a raccoon who's snatched a sweet piece.
"Can you spare a donut? This life is a quest!"
I hand over a muffin, and he's surely blessed.

A parrot squawks loudly, demanding my fries,
It seems even birds now have grown wise.
The waitstaff are characters, each with a flair,
"Don't leave without trying our famous stuffed bear!"

Chairs wobble like me, not quite in their place,
But laughter erupts as I make a new face.
"Is that a UFO?" a child boldly claims,
It's just my imagination playing silly games.

So here's to the stops with no signposts to find,
To mishaps that leave all the worries behind.
With whimsy as fuel and humor in tow,
Who says that the road has to follow a flow?

A Trail of What-ifs

What if I'd turned left, instead of the right?
Would I miss the parade of a raccoon delight?
Each twist of the wheel, a new story to tell,
In the land of confusion, I've learned to excel.

What if the mile markers could voice out their thoughts?
They'd giggle and chuckle, and lay down their knots.
With each silly turn, I'm grasping the fun,
Not knowing where I'm going, but here comes the sun!

What if I stopped asking, and just let it be?
To wander through life like a bumblebee?
Those worries are heavy, like bags full of rocks,
I'll scatter my doubts like I toss my socks.

So here's to the what-ifs that dance in the air,
To the joy of adventure found everywhere.
With laughter as compass, true treasures come forth,
In the chaos of travel, I've found my own worth.

Stuck in Traffic: A Soul's Odyssey

In a lane that's slow and steady,
Bumper to bumper, I'm feeling heady.
Missed my cue to take a ride,
As the universe has pushed aside.

GPS says to 'keep on track,'
But my sense of direction just won't come back.
A cow in pajamas is my new best friend,
And the honks from trucks never seem to end.

With coffee spilled on my favorite shirt,
I ponder life while stuck in this dirt.
Was that my exit? I can't quite tell,
As the radio plays a nostalgic swell.

The scenery shifts, but I'm still in place,
Waiting and wishing for some kind of grace.
The map's a jumble, it makes me laugh,
Maybe one day I'll find my own path.

The Unseen Crossroads

I stood at the fork, what a sight to see,
Two paths beckoned, but I was full of glee.
One promised joy, the other a snack,
I chose the donut, no way to look back.

Traffic lights flash like they're having a fit,
While I'm parked here, pondering my wit.
A squirrel steals my lunch, oh, what a crime!
Maybe life's punchline is lost in the grind.

Should I have turned? Oh, what a thought!
Maybe the exit's a battle I fought.
I chat with a tree, it gives me a charm,
In this wilderness, I find my own calm.

With mismatched socks, I make my way,
Each step an enigma, come what may.
The crossroads may shift, but don't catch a sigh,
I'll embrace the adventure, even as I'm awry.

Faded Maps of Ambition

My map's all crinkled, it's seen better days,
With coffee stains marking the lost highways.
I thought I was savvy, a traveler grand,
But I'm just a wanderer lost in no man's land.

Dreams like postcards, dusted with time,
Sent from the future, but oh, how they rhyme.
'Adventure awaits!' my friends all declared,
But on this ol' couch, I seem quite ensnared.

With a cat for a co-pilot, purring away,
My ambition's a hamster, so full of dismay.
We cruise through reruns, like an endless show,
As snacks make the journey a glorious flow.

I wave to the sky, with a wink and a grin,
As life's little humor settles under my skin.
The exit might vary, but here is my fate,
Wrapped in fine laughter, I patiently wait.

The Turn I Never Took

There was a moment, life took a spin,
An exit beckoned, but I chose to grin.
I thought I could drive, but I tripped on my shoes,
Now I'm stuck on this road, mismatched and confused.

The signs all giggle, 'you missed your chance!'
With traffic cones leading a playful dance.
I wave to the clouds, as they chuckle above,
Turns out this detour is just full of love.

With each mile marker, I craft a new plot,
Like a detective looking for clues I forgot.
My compass spins wildly, but it's simple and clear,
This ride's such a blast, I've got nothing to fear.

So here I am, making memories bold,
Life's an adventure, and it never gets old.
The turn that I missed, maybe it's all in jest,
In this winding road, I'm genuinely blessed.

Collisions of Paths and Possibilities

I took a turn too soon, oh dear,
Now I'm lost without a map near.
Traffic signs all look the same,
Wishing I could play this game.

GPS keeps yelling loud,
"Re-calculate!" - I feel cowed.
But I found a cafe on the way,
So maybe getting lost will pay.

I asked a squirrel for some help,
But he just offered me a yelp.
With a chuckle, I drive on,
In this wild ride, I'm never gone.

So many paths, a world of mess,
In confusion, I find some bliss.
Turning left and right I sway,
Life's missteps lead me here to stay.

Ghosts of Departed Destinations

The map is old, it creaks and moans,
Like ghosts entwined among the stones.
A detour here, a wrong-way sign,
Reminds me I'm not on the line.

My suitcase packed with dreams and snacks,
It's every ghost that I lack.
Chasing trails not meant to mine,
Is this a road or a punchline?

I call out loud to friends of yore,
"Are there tickets for exit door?"
They laugh and point to shadows long,
"Come join the dance; isn't it wrong?"

I'm haunted by the paths I missed,
In every twist, I clench my fist.
But here in limbo, I find the fun,
On this ride, I've truly won!

The Roundabout of Regrets

Round and round in dizzy spells,
Hitting every bump that yells.
I thought I'd find my exit fast,
Yet here I am, doomed to last.

Signals flashing, but who's to know?
I wave goodbye to chance's flow.
It's like a merry-go round of time,
With every beep, I lose my rhyme.

They say, "Just take the second turn!"
Yet here I spin, a lesson learned.
What's left behind is quite absurd,
Like lost keys in a giant bird.

But in this whirl, I laugh aloud,
No map can free me from this crowd.
So let's embrace this circular jest,
For here in muck, we're surely blessed.

Shadows in the Alley of Ambition

In darkened roads, my dreams collide,
With shadows lurking, unable to ride.
Ambition whispers, "Go ahead!"
I trip on laughter, scrape my head.

Every twist seems made of foam,
The alley leads me far from home.
But with a grin, I march along,
Shouting out my right to throng.

Who knew ambition could be so sly?
With every step, I laugh and cry.
The shadows dance, no need for fright,
In chaos here, I find delight.

So here I wander, lost but free,
In this alley where I can't see.
I'll mix my dreams with silly schemes,
And weave a path of joyful beams.

www.ingramcontent.com/pod-product-compliance
Lightning Source LLC
Chambersburg PA
CBHW051637160426
43209CB00004B/680